DREAMS AND JOURNEYS

DREAMS AND JOURNEYS

an esoteric relationship

Frederick McDonald

HARBOUR PUBLISHING

Harbour Publishing Co. Ltd.
P.O. Box 219, Madeira Park, BC, V0N 2H0
www.harbourpublishing.com

Edited by Peter Midgley
Cover and text design by Becky Pruitt MacKenney
Printed and bound in Canada
Printed on 100% recycled paper

Harbour Publishing acknowledges the support of the Canada Council for the Arts, the Government of Canada, and the Province of British Columbia through the BC Arts Council.

Library and Archives Canada Cataloguing in Publication

Title: Dreams & journeys / Frederick McDonald.
Other titles: Dreams and journeys
Names: McDonald, Frederick R., 1957- author.
Description: Poems.
Identifiers: Canadiana (print) 20220242852 | Canadiana (ebook) 20220242887 | ISBN 9781990776045 (softcover) | ISBN 9781990776052 (EPUB)
Classification: LCC PS8625.D6295 D74 2022 | DDC C811/.6—dc23

I dedicate this book to my daughters, Raven, Genny and Grace,
and to my grandchildren, Sebastian, Jewel, Johnny and Zoe.
Your unconditional love inspires….

Contents

9	Requiem for Darkness
12	Coffee....
16	Living in the Root Cellar
17	Grandpa's Canoe
19	Black and White
20	Rainbow Warrior
22	Inside of Dreams
23	Silent Scream
25	My Father's Old Mukluks
30	Johnny Cash Walks
31	Come Visit Me
33	The Invisible Sky
34	1 Brush Stoke
39	The Tree Dwellers
41	Sins of My Fathers
45	Dark Bavarian Chocolate
47	Our Languid Valley
50	The Magnifying Glass
58	The Silent Artist....
60	Light
61	Food for Ravens
62	The Last Request
65	Reconciliation / Conciliation
68	The Dark Hours
69	Crosses at the Crossroads
72	The End of the Trail
74	Two Ravens
78	The Biggest FIRE Ever!
82	From Hamburgers and Fries
84	In Our Kitchen
87	My Favourite Golf Course
89	A Stroke of the Brush

91   Don't Get Me Started

92   4 White Horses

94   By the Tailings Pond

96   My Own Private Hell....

97   Sometimes, the Darkness....

100   I've Lived the Best I Can

102   I Was Looking at a Painting

104   Jelly Jar Logic

106   Red Turns to Black

108   The Old Diner

112   Ghosts Along the Highway

114   Hot Pea Soup

115   Follow That Raven

116   My Living Area....

117   The Ice Skater....

118   Drive On, Walk On – Dream....

119   In a Turquoise World

120   Relentless....

127   Let's Talk

133   Acknowledgements

134   About the Author

Requiem for Darkness

his violin could be heard   wwwayyy-awfff

out where his music selections emanated from, as random
as those places he played, at times seemingly
nearby at an oddly placed cement well where
us kids gathered, making daily plans

lying above my sheets at the other side of a beautiful day
thinking about the day and wondering about
tomorrow   and tomorrow   and tomorrow

all those tomorrows that never came for him

imagining his pain
his
loneliness
his
sadness
drowning
in 26 ounces of Five Star Whisky

feeling his tormented soul through my open window

Mom and Dad spoke of him often after
those nights of listening to his violin
his soft, sad violin crying
even when i think about it now, his wife and child dying
a house fire taking them when he was away navigating
the river on a barge going north

everyone knew his story, the story of a man shrouded
in the absolute truths of life, with

only one thing left of his earthly dreams: death
but he was already dead.... dying in that fire

the beautiful sadness of the strings seemed at times accompanied by
a ghostly choir
2 voices from the
outlying dark shores of that river

one shore held the beauty of innocence and of a new bride
and a child, the other
the souls of the lost, forgotten by so many, many, many

his violin cries for him, he has no tears left
he speaks no more; he has nothing left to say
the air he breathes has no taste, no smell
the wind is the only thing he hears
and all he sees
a deep dark blue darkness
he feels nothing

his violin paints a hollow image of a desolate shadow
of a man already dead, wanting
that death
the only thing alive in him
his violin, unrequited reminiscence
a requiem for darkness, for
deaths, his included

for too long
for too long

he plays his death songs from one terrible lonely night to the next
his fingers move automatically, obscure motions
walking blindly drunk past those entangled roots   remembering
that same enchanted path when

he walked on those days of store-bought roses and homemade
    blueberry wine
his bride-to-be on his arm

i can still hear that violin crying in the melancholy
distance between life and death

one summer day when i was 10
i found him
at the bottom of our well,
his lifeless body floating beside
the violin

Coffee....

bacon and eggs sizzle and the coffee pot dances
Grandpa's got the pot-bellied stove just right
crackling wood consolidates the ancient perceptions
of our ancestors   they live right there in that one-room log
cabin amidst smells that awaken the day's possibilities
i roll over and watch him   he smiles at me
a twisting trail of his cigarette smoke causes him to partially
close one eye and his hands move deftly
placing the frying pan and coffee pot on the kitchen table
i ease myself up from my bed eager to meet the day
just like he's done for over three-quarters of a century
and pour myself a steaming fresh cup

the sound of coffee brewing
is drowned out by the morning news
it's pretty much the same on every channel, watching them all
trying to glean whatever i can, waiting
listening to what the experts have to say   talking about
peak oil or if Saudi Arabia, Iraq or Iran will flood the markets
affects decisions on how we manage to fulfill our contracts
the overhead, if not taken seriously, can kill
the sound of oatmeal gurgling in the pot softens the news
2 handfuls of frozen blueberries along
with frozen strawberries, mangoes, and peaches –
my morning ritual

the sound of the north wind plays alongside
those familiar songs that i've grown to love
songs that my grandfather loved, country music
i wonder if it all reminds him of her, my grandmother, whom
i've never met and interestingly enough he never talks about
the discussion that morning is of checking the traps at Coffee Lake

well, i'm the one who's going to check them
my grandpa isn't capable of walking the bush trails any longer
that distance through the -30° weather,
trying to balance on the narrow footpath is treacherous for him
the scales have tipped to me   he's giving me a few
last instructions before i head out   i slowly sip
hot coffee, building courage
to tackle winter's elements

i'm sitting in my comfy leather high-back chair
looking out at the river from my office
pondering my dad's family   i knew an uncle once
i wonder what he would have been like, had he lived
and it really sinks in that Grandpa never talked about his wife
i'm sure when he stared out the kitchen window at the river
he thought of her   he had that look, you know
the kind with a little twinkle in that one certain smile
the phone rings   i answer as i address the emails before me
it's going to be another busy day   my body and mind slip back
into the role of being the big boss, CEO
how i got here is pure cosmic energy caressed by a conspicuous
harmony of sneaking past the edge of a dark hole far out somewhere
in the universe, riding on solar flares in synchronization
with *them*, my ancestors

snowdrifts slide over their old path   walking is difficult
every now and again a foot slips off up to my knees in snow
snow has a way of creeping into my moccasins which irks me
        immensely
i hear him far behind me open the cabin door to feed his dogs
he keeps, mostly for nostalgic sentiments; 2 Ski-Doo Elans
transport us to and from town, even carrying a dog or 2 in their own
        sleighs
they love the ride and always, easily fall asleep
there's comfort in his soft gravelly voice as he
calls out each and every one of his dogs' names

i'm focused on the trail and without realizing it, his voice disappears
today i am hopeful that i will catch the Fisher that's
been sniffing around my traps and sets

my 8 o'clock has arrived and my assistant comes in
bringing coffee for us, though she knows that she doesn't
have to do that   she knows that i like it when she does
we sit down with our charts and reports discussing safety
stats, lateral friction, and if our margins have improved this month
consistently bouncing between 17 and 21 per cent
our discussions digress to a golf trip in 2 weeks' time
our yearly trip to Scottsdale with other CEOs, presidents, and owners
and the new drivers that we bought on sale at the end of last season
yet somehow my mind keeps slipping to the view outside
the north wind is pelting the window with fresh snow
sounding like Poe's Raven, invisible to the eye
but obvious to me, standing just outside my heart

the snares have done their job and my pack seems fuller
feet from 3 frozen hares stick out the top
the day has started well, excitement builds
as i get closer to the lake, expectations are high
i can see that the trap set has been disturbed
last time it was because of a lone wolf
stealing animals from my traps, knowing my routine
the deep brown fur still feels a bit warm as i carefully
place the Fisher beside the other catches of the day
i make a little fire to warm myself, pulling out
a couple bologna and bannock sandwiches   a celebration of sorts
they go wonderfully with the coffee Grandpa
put in his old Thermos   i sit looking at an open stretch
of that frozen isolated lake before me

eating my bologna and bannock sandwiches, lunchtime
in the quiet of the office   i can hear the murmur coming from
the other offices as i look out the window, something

i find myself doing way more these days, more than i should
my afternoon is going to be busy with the biweekly managers'
meeting starting at 1   i can hear the first few coming up the stairs
there's a confident air in their voices, numbers have been good
TRIF is down and the bottom line is up
the wind knocks at my window, and i realize i've been
hypnotized by the past again, staring out my window
i take one more look north up to the farthest bend in the river
i grab my coffee, head into the boardroom

Living in the Root Cellar

living
in the root cellar
in a room hastily built
for a growing teenage boy
just below the kitchen
the smell of damp earth is mixed
in with bacon, eggs, and coffee
"breakfast is ready," i hear my mom's call
then the thunder of little steps
of my brothers and sister and the odd
friend who just happened by for coffee
tapping his foot to Johnny Cash
playing on our Electrohome console stereo
my father sitting in the living room
smoking a Player's Light cigarette
sounds and smells from upstairs
entering my bloodstream
flowing along with the familiar
amalgamating in an adolescent
and sensual way with the
earth

Grandpa's Canoe

that little 14' canoe that
my grandpa owned floats effortlessly in
the rivers of my heart
      ssshhwooosh

green paint chipped exposing red paint
underneath, then blue and bits of grey
like a layered birthday cake
      sshhwooohhhp

bumps and squared edges show
where repairs were made, random
as those accidents that caused them
      kllluupoooluuunk

inside, the ribs are worn clearly
showing its age; if you're not careful you will
get splinters in your knees and feet
      sshhpwuuukassooops

bits of different-coloured rope show where
loads had been tied into
gunnels that are chipped, split, and broken
      sshhpoink

blood is congealed to the walls, splattered
Rorschach test patterns from fish, ducks, geese
beavers, deer, moose, and other animals
      sshpoooshh

i hear water lapping against the canvas in a Morse code of sorts
rhythms that calm my soul and ease

my mind, i'm smiling now
        ssh palll ooossh hssooo lllap hss

i remember well, he taught me how
to hold and handle the paddle, pull the water
use J-strokes in ways so as not to tip
        shhhaawooosh

2 paddles, 1 shorter, seldom matched, usually
stored by each seat, keep a clean edge; Grandpa says
push out from bank using the handle
        phsshguulooog ahhh

there are no life jackets as
this is a time before that time, but there is
a single-shot shotgun and an old Lee–Enfield 303
        sshwooosh kaaplooo – kaaplooohhh

keep the weight low in the canoe
to lower the centre of gravity, especially when
it's windy or in a current fast and strong
        buuurgully shpaahlooosh

stories are etched and scratched into its wood and
canvas body with similar scars that come from parts of
my grandfather's own story
        sshhwooohhhp

i remember the times we spent and places we went   fun
·that little 14' canoe drifts and remains
largely elements of me
        ssshwwooooshhh

Black and White

black and white photographs
of where a boy became a man

evoke emotions in full CinemaScope
sensory-overloaded familial projections

of parents a party to dysfunction
memories of them defined and colourful

the dented brownish two-toned half-ton Ford
parked beside a growing pile of lumber scraps

the tarpaper garage full of tools and junk
that us boys borrowed whenever we liked

the backyard littered with bits and pieces
memories and hope flood over to the front

Ravens float above dogs in wired pens
croaks and barks echo musically in cranial valleys

nostalgia overwhelms with these images
even the ones that show our house flooded

the kitchen window is open and i smell supper cooking
i hear my mom and dad talking with my brothers

all sitting around a kitchen table
strong enough to dance on

Rainbow Warrior

out of the blackness
rode the rainbow warrior
on a large white steed 20 hands high
seething out its mouth   blackened froth
steam   100°C blasting from its nostrils
turning, running away, going nowhere
an appalling dream   protesting
environmental destruction   365 of us yelling
at mirrored corporate windows
within the downtown of hundreds of other corporations
our voices echoing down avenues of concrete
buildings reaching up to the sky
blocking out the sun
all of us standing in eternal greyness   within their shadowlands
sucking the energy out of me, out of them
living, working in their zombie world
dark hollowed-out eye sockets
hands cuffed with golden zip ties   self-tied
manipulated by the newest world order
sad

the black portal
from which the steed burst closes
a flash of black light   negative energy
from a black hole   power of a thousand galaxies
the unbearable thunder of osmium-shod hooves
galloping across time with memories of   colonization
a handsome powerful Indigenous warrior
black Raven hair braided and tied   prepared for war
leading the charge into the battle
answering the call for a true leader
needed   animals and plants are dying

rivers are drying and the planet is   burning up
where   racism is rampant
politicians spew vapid unintelligible   noise
lacking what most is needed   honour
their lies paving their way to the next election
speeding across lakes of molecular indiscretions
their wakes drowning reason

powerful flashes of lightning
strike the base of those transitory towers
as Conquest skids   stopping
in front of   corporate   ominous   structures
yet, still dreaming a call to action is met
thousands stand in solidarity
voices rise and a call for leadership   true leadership
governments flounder   angst and nervousness prevail
requiring definitions and direction
i'm still running getting nowhere
and now i'm starting to float
up with others   we watch the rainbow warrior
enter building upon building as ground floors   explode
shards of glass fly into the streets
while animated police goon squads   ineptly beat the activists back
doing the dirty work of so-called 'right honourable' politicians
whom we've elected   right or wrong
doing their bidding not ours   partisan politics
civil war ensues
anarchy

Inside of Dreams

i travel inside of dreams across
platitudes of the surreal
searching for those good intentions
creating heaven
a voice bellows from   out there
a portal opens in a kitchen
Mom's heavenly delights of
moose meat and bannock cooking
the older pretty teen girl next door has 'Pretty Woman' blaring
heaven exists over her fence
the familiar sound of a truck door
slamming and a boy flying up the porch steps
the front door flies open
the eternal question on his lips: "is supper ready?"
a robin whistles, perched on a branch 23' from the corner of the house
somewhere beyond, Prometheus is talking to Coyote
planning a heavenly takeover
sliding out of dream state thinking i should remember this
this promise of a good dream

Silent Scream

suffering through colonial pages of time
confused over the effects of views
of "another's" cultural perspective
weighing profoundly upon my people

i scream, silent at the words
trying to reach back to those historians
who referenced research and subsequently
to those writers of that research

i look to them to explain, perhaps
at this time, "they" may try to defend
the hudson's bay company selling
"rupert's land" to canada

i question the hbc ownership of said land
steal the land, take it yelled the conjurors
the silent subjugation of the original inhabitants
the silent bewilderment is deafening

i also question whether that purchase
gave the sale some sort of credibility
of course, it was recorded, it's in "the books"
"it" conforms to "their" legalities of accountability

a dominion of corrupt politicians
taking advantage of a situation
extrapolated profits in multiple dimensions
personal – for "themselves" and "their" friends

of course, that's all conjecture i suspect
based on what happens, even now

the lawyers for the crown will have "their" say
in a court designed by "those who" have the most to lose

the stealing continues, of land and resources
through policies and legislation changing
policies and legislation, makes it all
confusing, ingeniously designed

government lawyers jam the courts
judicial systems protect those who design the system
indiscretion and injustice reign, win the day

the silent scream in my head gets louder, grows
and i rage at the words with words, colonized
but "their" words can be used,
will be used

the silence will be heard

My Father's Old Mukluks

the distant rising sun emits
long and short wavelengths diffused
refractions of stories, theirs, urgent
subatomic messages permeate my soul

my father's old mukluks
sit, kind of hiding – waiting
on a shelf in the study / office
on the other side of the house

keeping them there, feeling
a sense of paternal connection – like he's still alive

they are in an old brown
Red & White grocery bag
stored for 4 decades, approximately
in 4 different homes, always in the same place:
on a shelf in a room never far from where
there's a place to think
where i dream

dreams
pour over the horizon,
fall off the edge of the world

northern lights speak to me
the north star calls
the world taunts me – again and again and again
ripping my soul apart

that day arrived
convocation ceremony's about to start

Mother and Father have travelled
the 800 km, adding
to the specialness of the occasion

this day began 5 years earlier, when
after travelling halfway around the world
realization set in that something needed to be done, something
different than what sent me
searching through conjunctures
travelling through the darkness, then
returning each time, lights flickering

craziness led to fear of the mundane
repetitivity leading to instability

precarious dreams relative to life
dreams of a young man, old

i remember telling them
i was leaving, heading out
going to the other side of the world
going to a place that lived only
in books and movies
in dreams

Australia called like a banshee with cherry-red lipstick,
blue-green eyes and a fine, shapely figure

a Norwegian i knew said that he threw a dart
at a map of canada and that's how he ended up
living with Grandfather, trapping and hunting
enticing story, arousing dreams, soaring in me

i threw my dart

the trade of trapping   i learnt from them all

reading serious selections in high school
confusing – guided / inspired by a pretty, slight, young
English teacher with big blue eyes
and short straight dirty-blond hair
5 years older, recommended reading material
smitten, was I, by books and her

i found out years later that Mom cried
she did not understand   i left with my soul – barely alive

when she died, i found a box of photographs
she had saved for just herself   i imagined
her smiling, looking at them, at us as kids

Huckleberry Finn talks to me
i feel the passion of Pierre Bezukhov
see the desires and hopes of Odysseus
the frustrations of Jake Barnes
i laugh with the brash Crocodile Dundee

dreams so big that no
coliseum could quarter them nor
any hometown hold me

i did not know it then, my ancestors prompted me to leave

Honolulu, Fiji,
Sydney, Hobart, Perth, the Great Barrier Reef
Auckland, Palmerston North,
LA, Toronto, New York, Cancun, Mexico City and finally
Austin and Calgary – almost 2 years

halfway round the world, living
half a lifetime in those few years

oh, there are many stories alive

in all those town and cities
along all those highways and byways
and back roads
on those mountains, beaches, and reefs
and of course, in those resorts, hotels, hostels,
cafes and bars

lifetimes of experiences and education

books led to dreams
led to travel, to contemplation
led me to find me

on a day in 120° Fahrenheit weather
with 85% humidity, a cold chill overwhelmed me
i realized something concrete
was the only answer to life

abstract dreams
became reality

after being a road warrior / scholar
now a student / academic
living / working the ultimate dream

the day had come
years of study – finished
the hour was upon
standing before the world
diploma in hand
Eagle feather in the other
and wearing Dad's mukluks
i step out into the noonday sun

dreams followed   through

a truest sense of it all
it was their dream too, Mom and Dad's

my father's old mukluks sit
beside Mom's box of old photographs

sun rises above that horizon
i sit with coffee in what is now my studio
not far from them

diffractions of light slip through dreams

Johnny Cash Walks

Johnny Cash, you walk through my head
wearing your black suit, with a white shirt
and that twisted, painful smile

each step arouses in a sort of feathered
rhythm of hidden meadowlarks and
boisterous murders of crows

your songs remind me of life
lived right to the edge of death
resonating through my community

where is the joyful pitter-patter of children?
where are the balanced soliloquys of the living?
it's interesting though how i love your extremes

prison, cocaine, needles and crazy
permeate society's lost souls
and society itself

desperadoes, ghost riders, and a boy named Sue
sing beside and along with you   Kris, Waylon and Willie
touching the eternal hopefulness in all of us

you are an inspiration
you've seen the devil's darkest fires
and God's eternal light

Come Visit Me

when your plane touches down, come visit, it'd be nice
to see you, rent a car, catch a cab or call a friend, come by

at the end of the airport road, hang a right, go past that first
industrial park and after the streetlights, go down the hill, enjoy

the view, pretty nice where 2 rivers meet every day, no matter what
come as you are and for fun wear a bowler or an Irish tweed, if you
    wish, but

come, head north through town, follow safely behind the big trucks
    but not too
close, all are headed the same way, going to one site or other; there's

a few traffic interchanges, drive by them all, don't turn off, not left nor
right, go straight, turn on some tunes, maybe the Eagles, Beatles or

Animals, after passing the next industrial park, you're on the right
    track, drive
for 45 minutes, enjoy the views, yes there are more, they're different

than normal – industrial turns lead to humongous oil plants   don't
take them and try not to breathe; the airborne hydrocarbons will tickle

your throat   when you get to the stoplights that seem out of place
dear friend, veer left, but watch for speeding tractor-trailers, go

safely through and then around, don't stop at our industrial park, on the
left   watch for turning trucks and equipment, go across the bridge and

up the hill   be careful of kids and of those pesky road bumps, go
past a few single-wide trailers and similar-looking condos, bookended

by mostly new 3-bedroom bungalows
with quads and snowmobiles in the
front yards and even a rusty car or truck, behind a brand new one or two

along the top edge of an unassuming cliff
above our friendly looking river
enjoy that view too; it's pretty damn nice   well, i love it   i'm sure i'm not

the only one, then down a slight slope passing the community store
   and our administration building that's across from the radio
   communication tower

with all the newest gadgetry of technological confabulations and just
beyond there's the school up on a slight rise to the left

next to the new youth centre and hockey arena, drive cautiously through
this area, and hey that's where my brother used to live, but

he no longer lives, there, at the first 4-way intersection turn left
but watch for the pothole, go over it; it's nasty, take the third left

and there amongst some trees is my grey-coloured home, with the large
windows   i'll probably see you coming
drive up the narrow driveway, mind

the ditch; it's a bitch   walk up the stairs and knock softly on the door
   if i'm not
already on the deck, i'll answer, probably in my pjs
with paint on the knees

i'll be so happy that you did....

The Invisible Sky

natural spring water
oozes from the earth, floating insects struggle
soon dead, drowning in the purest sense

falling leaves
soak into a darkened earth, tantalizingly delicious
centipedes and earthworms dance in roundabout ways

there's a smell of rain in the air

a figure pronates
by rotten trees, eats a bologna sandwich
has an internal discussion on climate change

phantasmagorical clouds
filtered through the autumn's foliage

float unnoticed overhead, speak

no words, no language
just leaves and branches and time, surround me
i take it all in, touch my eternal soul

hovering again above the trees
no one sees me
looking at the invisible sky

1 Brush Stoke

life comes to the fore

18 years in the bush – young years
living with and off and on the land and water
spirits heard, sounds – unnerving, it's all good i tell myself
hunting, trapping, and fishing
bannock, bologna and moose meat sandwiches
boreal conversations – voices in my head

variations on themes of deep forest and emerald greens

14 years in construction
red seal interprovincial ticket – 4 years
safety, gas detection, team health and other industrial-sized programs
pulling wrenches in the dust and grime and tastes of hydrocarbons all
    the time
my spirit died, that's no lie – i had no choice but to fly

fly from black coke dust to cobalt blue skies

on to 2 years living out of a backpack
sleeping in ditches, in farmer's fields, in forests
and in Sally Anns, halfway houses, hostels and even a graveyard (once)
all of them equally eerie
along lonely stretches of the trans-canada highway
in and out of similar places in faraway countries

forlorn rainbows – colours no one can touch

6 months down under
on the Great Barrier Reef – 4 weeks of

fishes, sharks, eels, and whales
then oscillating softly on the top deck, touching the Milky Way

phthalocyanine and cerulean blue nights dotted with starry, starry lights

8 years of university
painting and literature, and canadian and First Nations studies
Aboriginal associations and rainforest action groups
socio-political, religious, and environmental injustices

cadmium medium red and naphthol crimson days

then 4 tough CEO years
working with the visions of others
leading meetings, strategic plans, contract and project management
    and stress
stress and managers, supervisors, frontline workers and contract holders

black and blue egos seen through bloodshot weary eyes

numerous road trips across canada and the states
2 territories, 10 provinces and 48 states
6 months in Austin, New York – 10 times (my absolute favourite)
i'll happily share stories – with a nice glass of a house red

Naples yellow ignites red oxide – suddenly i'm on fire

500 plus paintings complete in 50 plus exhibitions
all because of one *Old Mike*
hanging on a lonely wall in a busy gallery

sentimental colours of my people .

2 weeks in Mexico City, 1 in Guadalajara
getting lost on my way to Teotihuacan
between slums and people dying on the streets

studying ruins and nearly lost codices
the mural masters show me a way

burnt umber and blood red paths of my ancestors

Vincent, and Arthur Shilling
light the fire, passions burning

golden fields filled with black crows and reddish-brown faces

Dali, Picasso, Claude, Camille and Degas
Leonardo, Michelangelo, Rafael, Caravaggio and Botticelli
candlelight from across time illuminates a path for me
Rivera, Siqueiros, Orozco and yes, of course.... Frida
Tom, Franklin, Frederick Varley, Lawren and Emily
ignite and inspire
Norval, Alex, Jackson, Daphne, Bill and Joane Cardinal-Schubert
Jane, Jim Logan, Leanne, Garry, Pierre, Phil and Paul
have stories that burn inside of me

influences, all of them
adding narrative to voice

voices resonating through holes in time
realities of probability resonate with possibility

positive and negative spaces and colours fill our dreams

Robert, Edgar, W. Whitman, W.C. Williams, W.B. Yeats and W.
    Shakespeare
walk through time to touch my hand
E. Pauline, Louise, Lee Maracle and Maria Campbell
Chief Dan George, Richard, Drew, Tom and James Welch
breaking barriers with every page, every word
Homer, Uris, Alistair, Orwell and good ole Count Leo
J.R.R., F. Herbert, Anne McCaffrey, Steinbeck and Twain

Bilbo, Frodo and Samwise, Tom Joad and Huckleberry Finn
destinies that guide my soul

words, visions destined for blank sheets

Robby, Winston, Buffy, A. Napoleon Sunchild and Rita Coolidge
heart songs that lift our people
Elvis, Frank, Leonard, Croce, Springsteen, Stevie Ray and Sam
Johnny, Willie, Kris, George, Linda, Karen, Olivia and Eva
Abraham, Martin, John, Bobby and Diana
time tries but can't erase their voices

generational rhythms between edified genres

Roland, Rick, Grandpa Harry, Mom and Dad
Dorothy, Ruby Ann, Elsie, Norman and Basil
Billy, John, Lambert, Danny, Dana and Ernest
it seems like family and friends pass more often these days
their stories becoming my stories

inevitability – black holes extricating all kinds of colour until all is
    pure white

my children and my grandchildren
carrying the lights of all
they begin their own journeys

spring, sun's rising, yellows leading to reds – ahhhh

then there's that "1 thing"
leaving the great thinkers mystified
about the beginning of time, and the ends of it too
O, C, H and N and all the other elements
earth, water, air, fire, food and space

creation

too damn much to comprehend
too many to mention
all leading to some kind of justifiable moment
lifetimes leading back to Socrates
and to the Great Spirit

i've become the colour of each

with every breath and thought
with every image and design
it all starts with

1 brush stroke

The Tree Dwellers

there's a secret code amongst the tree dwellers,
i was told not to share this until it was time,
i am the last; they left me to find another home

i'm half human and they, well it's hard to explain
their wings translucent, almost invisible
are tinged with touches of emerald green and cobalt blue

some may say it's just imagination,
just a collection of false memories,
something dreamt

but for those who don't believe,
we must just let that be for now
perhaps those curiosities have long since faded

yet, the legends grew of the creatures who loved the trees,
people came from across the world to visit
even from other star systems; multitudes

my home, on a high ridge of this lonely mountain, 'bout halfway
difficult to get to, to find, but still they come,
many questions, but there's always one i never answer

i never saw a good enough reason
they came seeking something they hadn't earned
why should i give them the last thing that was truly mine?

yes, i too question why they left
why there is little of that magic left in the trees
sadly, i see the trees disappearing, quietly

if they are willing to sacrifice the beauty
the sacred, ancient magic in these trees,
i wonder to what other lengths they might go

it scares me, this powerful wind of change in the air
yet i still do not understand the depth of nature
the true beauty and balance that it represents

and i heard the tree dwellers continue to fight,
stretching themselves thin searching for any hope
but to some beings, their own glory is more important

questions are a curious preoccupation
to peoples and entities of difference, leading to others
always looking for that one great answer

Sins of My Fathers

sins of my father, barely perceptible
memories torn from a worn-out tapestry
that hung in a dimly lit corner
of our smoke-filled living room
i came to know it was similar to those huge historic ones
prodigiously hanging in the light-sensitive sections
of New York City's Metropolitan Museum of Art

the tapestry's image has disintegrated
from years of electromagnetic impulses
the silver oxide shadows of sins
originating in the farthest fields of my mind
floating between the pupil and the optic nerve
conjuring thoughts of my youthful father
at any given or desired moment

his sins have carried me
down gravelly roads
that i no longer want to travel
and into backrooms
where i sometimes find myself
sitting in his darkness
sometimes waking in the arms
of women i do not know
similar to those times i heard
what my father may have done in his day

he's been on my mind
consciously and unconsciously
consistently since his passing, yet there's
a part of my body no longer
wanting to feel those old

familiar pangs nor pieces of angst
remembered moments of rants, raging
at the historical indiscretions
of governmental Aboriginal policies abused
and changed, whims
of dim-witted politicians
coming and going
election after election
portfolio changes and
departmental directions blown callously apart
verbal injustices and dirges
of two-faced, white-skinned monkeys
ancient, time-stained rhetoric
of liberal or conservative ideologies
fabricated election promises
that i heard my father
discussing in many of his drunken tirades
as he would say are the sins
of the fathers of those careless politicians

at 8½ years i remember
looking through a cracked window of
my grandfather's old trapline cabin
with one particular midnight campfire's
light reflecting off
my father's delightful face
in a brilliant blaze of yellow-red hues
behind the dancing silhouettes of his friends
as various lengths of pine and poplar logs
burn with that predictable exothermic reaction
sparks mixing with the stars in the heavens above
i hear him telling stories
muffled reminiscences
incoherent words in a kind of secret code
fabricated within the heated moments of
those tales of adventures and misadventures

beside that great river
belonging to them and now
belonging to our river

yes, i could say the sins are many
but, considering the many kinds
of social preoccupations, visceral fascinations
and religious implications
making my head spin
trying to elucidate within that circle of familial rage
the sins of my father or
the sins of his father or
the sins of all fathers

i feel reconstituted sins of weeks
when he left my mother behind
and with that, us too
perhaps the greatest sin of all
to go on those binges of
cigarettes, beer, and women
stories we heard about

true or not, they are out there
sadness fills my heart
beating with the sadness of his heart
repressed explorations
repressed explanations
unexplained feelings of his mother, lost to disease and
an inconsolable father remaining behind
that time has unmercifully selected

within a personal osmosis of sorts
they too have become mine

visible, in that old tapestry
hanging in the farthest corner of

of the back reaches of my mind
in the second to last room
are the sins of my father
sitting on a dusty shelf
in an old rusty frame, a family portrait
directly across, 24' from Christ on his cross
and after all of his transgressions
i don't blame him; all that i have left....

forgiveness

Dark Bavarian Chocolate

the dark Bavarian chocolate tasted wonderful,
the one i bought earlier, to celebrate today

my walk feels good as the late winter sun is setting,
snow is melting, the soft crunching with each step is music

off to my left Ravens play tag with a neighbourhood dog,
stealing his steaming hot food   i watch, thinking, they're jerking his
    chain

a symbiotic relationship that makes everything feel like life is good,
like when the sun is shining and it's -35 and i'm driving a back-
    country bush road

thoughts drift to yesterday's sun descending into that icy starry night,
something that my friends, Vincent, Salvador, Robert and Edgar,
    would have loved

alone, within the magnificence of the Milky Way, on one of my
    favourite lakes,
i feel my ancestors watching me   they are saying something
    whispers fill the air

without any notice, there's a rush of wind, blowing out of nowhere,
a mini tornado of sorts swirls around me   as quick as it came, it's gone

that's when i notice one red star, slightly brighter than the rest,
it could be my grandfather   something tells me it is him, smiling

to my right, i see a hint of aurora borealis, the light show just
    beginning,
just above the horizon, delineating then and tomorrow

i've become hypnotized by the tempo of my steps, vaguely aware,
each breath producing visible exhalations, freezing, fogging my glasses

i take them off   in the distance, i see my front door light flickering,
my pace quickens as the chill of my long walk has finally caught up

i close the door, slowly take off my heavy-ish down-filled coat
warm water washes away the icicles crystallized on my moustache

sighing easily, feeling satisfied, i sink into my supple couch,
place a glass of fruity cabernet sauvignon, my favourite, on the side table

through my living room windows, i watch car headlights streak by,
and far behind that nocturnal scene, are their stars, heavenly,
    beckoning me

i put my head back, the dark Bavarian chocolate tastes wonderful,
the one i bought earlier, to celebrate today

Our Languid Valley

growing up in that languid green valley,
that long, lazy, not-so-deep lively valley,
at the confluence of 3 rivers
on the edge of the ethereal
of a somewhat convergence of reality
where a world of brown allegories meets white parables
in a communal sense of righteousness
with God entering our souls every Sunday
in a white wooden church, with a white steeple,
with wide white stairs above white lattice,
with white framed windows
through which light streams

a foreign pretense of fine stained glass ordered
from far afield to its now dusty resting place
captured the imagination of a young "Indian" boy
hoping to catch a glimpse of God in those magical hues
of blue, yellow and red, those browns and greens and royal purples,

compositions straight from the pages of our family bible,
fill the church hall, reflect
off the walls, floors, pews and backs of heads of many other little boys
dreaming of summer things like swimming and fishing,
and adventures of Huckleberry Finn and Tom Sawyer,
searching the faces and sides of faces
of the adult congregation sitting dutifully
praising God's graciousness and all-seeing power,
wearing their finest haberdasheries ordered
from either the Simpsons, Sears or Eaton's catalogues,
selected while in each of their own, differing states of stoned stasis,
from closets filled with new clothes and sun-bleached skeletons,

despite the pilsner or whisky hangovers,
amid the not-so-distant echoes of whoops and hollers
that resonate long after the rising summer sun
put an end to the party next door,
the church is filled with family and friends and
people who've come north looking for work
and staying because in some mysterious benevolence
they felt at home, friendships
transcending different cultures and countries
and millions of light years

only to come to rest
on this ground at their feet

it opens up to an internment of happiness
sucking them in, down into a
congenial, contemporaneous social hypnotic abyss
as they sit underneath
big, wonder-filled poplar trees, drinking tea
or other refreshing not-so-similar kinds of drinks
talking about who knows what
while i ran by wondering what they were
saying, debating or discussing
perhaps something about
The Athabascan, a large barge that is just
disappearing in the distance around a long, hazy bend
of that ancient river, my river, like i've said so many times,
that i watched earlier and many times before, wondering where it goes
carrying fuel and food for mythic northern settlements,
laden with memories of fur trappers,
Cree, Dene, Chippewa and Métis
whose furs filled the storage holes and containers
of many such barges
memories mixed with Scottish, French and Irish fur trader's wares

the ringing of the three little, golden bells my buddy is shaking –
he is this week's altar boy, wearing a clean white robe,
the one i wore last Sunday –
brings me back to what the priest is saying in Latin
i sit in my clean Sunday best denim jeans
with my best white Sunday going-to-mass shirt
i wear my scuffed Oxford dress shoes
that have grown tight and uncomfortable,
not really listening to the sermon,
just daydreaming, like i am now,
caught in an effervescent downtown high-rise
in a big city miles and miles and years away
passing
like so many family and friends
now lying amongst the roots of pine and poplar trees,
in our old graveyard, on that little knoll,
in the middle of our languid valley....

The Magnifying Glass

chapter 1….

the magnifying glass
caused a stir in my imagination
refractions of life between here
and there
looking through this magical prism
held me captive to thoughts
of the prospect of proving
that what we read was true
that the sun's light   could start a fire

the day was like any other
hot summer day, and
for 2 brown, bubbly boys
mischievous, inquisitive boys
it was perfect

Mom and 6 of her friends
were inside our neighbour's old, modest log cabin
having a tea party and making bannock
i was told to stay outside, but stay in view

reflecting now on this moment
pulls me back through that glass

on a narrow path, through
a big yard of dry grasses
boys are hunched, cuddled together
slight shoulder movements, almost imperceptible
moving a magnified light to its apex
the tiny point of white heat

focused on the little pile of dry grass
on that narrow path

the voices of Mom and her friends
resemble the distant blur of the sounds
of chickens and hens
mixed in with laughter
lively, womanly laughter

i think now.... how wonderful

before too long
a wee fire started
following the training
received from our fathers
we added more grass

we piled it on so it wouldn't go out
and 2 little boys – 10 years old
were as giddy as the women
in the cabin beside the little fire
on a narrow path in a good field of dry grasses

we did our own rendition of chickens
running around, pecking
bobbing up and down
grabbing grasses to stoke the fire

well, 2 little boys
stamped on the flames
4 little Indian feet doing a war dance
danced around, stamping the ground

the fire roared
the smoke billowed black
it rose to the heavens

it darkened the sky
it grew and grew
it grew out of control

"holy fuck – what next?"
(yes, we were well versed in all the best expletives)

run and hide
then, blame this on someone else?
that would never fly

what do we do?

so, i did the only thing that would save our skin
that would save the field of grass
that would save the cabin
that would save the forest
i ran in the open door and yelled....

F I R E !

chapter 2....

my mother and her friends ran out
like a bunch of mother hens
even in light of the seriousness of the situation

i saw the whole scene like a Saturday afternoon cartoon
i chuckled
just like i'm chuckling now

and even when light years have passed through
to the other side of that prism, i'll probably still chuckle
observing the absurdity of it all

out they came
out of the cabin
one with a broom
one with a mop
one with a pillow
one with a towel
one with a wool blanket

one grabbed a shovel that leaned against the house
one grabbed a rake that lay on the ground
out they ran, weaved and bobbed
squawking, like scaredy-cat chickens

what should i do?

run, hide, watch, stay out of the way?
i chose the only right thing – i jumped to it
i fought the fire too
we all fought hard
scrambled here, stampeded there
all of us doing a fire dance

i looked around   my friend had disappeared
i was on my own, well, kind of – you know what i mean

so now, sit back and imagine this....
a bunch of well-dressed women
in their finest summer dresses
flowered dresses
red and yellow dresses
white dresses
and me, dressed like Huckleberry Finn
we were all doing the....
put-out-the-fire dance

as i think back – i chuckle....

the fire got out of control
it grew and grew
no matter what we all tried to do
it grew and grew

then it hit me
it was headed for the forest
running wildly for the forest
ahead of us – around us
right to the forest

i remember thinking
we can't let that happen!
the forest will burn down, and i know for sure
if the fire burns it down
my ass is gonna burn too
like hell, fire and brimstone
my ass is gonna burn, burn, burn

we all stamped on the ground like the crazy drunk
that hung out at our town's only tavern
Mom was yelling and her friends were yelling
it sounded like an "Indian War Song"
it looked all like an "Indian War Dance"
straight outta a B western
we all danced at the edge of
that growing fire

it grew and grew
it moved faster and i imagined
what was next
the forest would burn to the ground
and all i could think was
my ass is gonna burn down too

i remember all this like it was just hours ago

i put my back into it
i put my whole body into full-speed-ahead
i was a bee scurrying from red rose to red rose
i was a butterfly
i was the town drunk
i probably felt like him too
i wished this would go away
i wished it was a dream – no, not this bad dream

the glass strikes again, a flash of light – i'm back

it was a beautiful summer day
and the smoke filled the sky
the smoke filled our lungs
the smoke stuck to our clothes
and our clothes turned black
as black as the smoke blocking the sun

the fire burned and burned
the smoke billowed,
flames burned red
it reached the forest
but through the dense smoke
my mom's friends had spread out
their stamping and shovelling
and raking and towel and blanket and pillow flicking
had done the job
the fire was out
it was a smouldering black mess

all eyes turned to me
i can still feel those eyes
those burning eyes

it was just then i had this funny thought
i don't have to cut the grass this weekend

at that moment
the Fire Department showed up
they checked everything
just to make sure
and yes, it was out
the magnificent 7 women
and the precocious little brown boy
who were all chimney-stack black
had put the fire out

but
that was not the end of it

chapter 3....

the women all gave me a
tongue-lashing
the Fire Department chief gave me   the talk
but my mom's look said it best
it was her look that worried me the most
all i could think: my butt was gonna burn

when everyone left
and only the two of us stood there
looking at my deconstructed creation
my mom said: go into the bush and get a willow
not a little willow
not a tiny, teeny-weeny willow
get a good sized one
get the right sized one and
if you don't – it'll be worse for you!

of course, another funny thought plopped into my head
my backside, my back or my butt, or both?

and again, being who i am
the first branch was an itsy-bitsy one – 6" long
held between my right thumb and index finger
the next was twice that size
the third was not much larger
the fourth was getting closer
closer, but not fast enough – my mom was getting madder
and i knew my butt was gonna burn, bad, then badder
i continued to delay the inevitable

to say the least
i finally got the right size
it took about a half hour
it wasn't a willow, no – no
that wouldn't do
i had found the perfect butt beater
it looked like a rapier
from *The Scarlet Pimpernel*

as i slip back and forth through that glass
magnified in times and places
to say the least
that back then – my butt burned
for two days
my butt burned like the fire i started

and.... i deserved it!

The Silent Artist....

sediment in the water, agitated by time

i travel
through oily stains on a liquid highway,
seeing, when looking up from within my shadow –
rising consequences

bending, and at times turning sunlight and starlight into
colours in compositions of time

navigating through time,
speaking of journeys,
like that's not been said before,
the night reluctantly becomes day,
light, without silhouettes

the water constantly turns to rust,
each moment never-ending   ethereal thoughts, stuck
crystals form, chemical changes take place,
take time   remember,
the Creator has been telling me – share the stories....

there is the artist, silent – painting.

oh, how i long for those warm summer days,
fields of grass growing tall, where i walked,
forests, many hues of green and animals, unseen,
my favourite river, a constant in this landscape,
(i thank Creator for that)
big skies, big clouds, thunderous and passionate blues,
the sun rising golden, then setting in a blazing reddish ball

melancholia overwhelms me, sadness
at the thought of conversations i could have had with Vincent
and at the thought of my friend alone in that field,
with those crows and some brushes and paint and a gun,
a little crazy, perhaps, but sometimes we all are

Light

sun

light
filtering through grey clouds,
dark clouds,
dark blue clouds,
loud clouds – thunder-filled,
moving on treetops,
touching tree tips,
slipping over trees,
over forests,
shapes,
shapes moving,
spiritual shapes,
multi-dimensional shapes,
funny looking shapes,
sometimes they look like something shapes,
moving quickly – touching
as many trees as possible,
i'm mesmerized – again for the
4th time today,
doesn't seem fair
i'm the happiest person
in the world in those moments,
moments – touching moments,
touching – here,
touches my heart,
touches – me....

Food for Ravens

i've been putting food
on my deck for the Ravens
every other day
for the past few weeks
mostly on really cold days, like today

now i've noticed
that they fly by
every other day
like today
to check to see if i put some food out for them

they must know that i love them
and when they fly by
looking for food
sometimes it looks just like
they are flying by just to say – hello!

The Last Request

the saddle was well worn,
a deep translucent brown on
a navy-blue blanket, with red trim,
it had been made for Billy Joe's palomino,
whose coloration was especially beautiful
on that sunny day with the backdrop of heavy clouds
hanging over the Grand Tetons

Billy mounted in one single harmonious movement
Bella Coola was especially excited
because she sensed today, as they did once a year,
they'd be going into the back country

Bella had been Billy's 16th birthday present
Bella's name coming from her father's favourite fishing spot
now – together, best friends for 10½ years,
a match made in heaven, that day

tomorrow was her father's birthday and as a special treat
Billy and Bella were making a long weekend journey
to his most special place in the world

their cabin was on a sharp bend on the Snake River,
a secret place far enough away from the hordes
where her father would always say,
        "a man could hear himself think,"
after a few years, he changed it to:
        "where a father and a daughter...."

the two of them had been going there for 15 years

everyone was worried for her – but she was confident

she had had the best teacher
and at her side the Marlin 1894 lever-action
Dad gave her when she started taking long rides alone
it was light enough for her to handle,
with enough power to take down a grizz,
if the need arose

the words of her father always in her mind:
'put the stock firm against your cheek
and make sure the butt is firm against your shoulder'
it had a good firm kick – it packed a punch
the first time she shot it she landed on her butt
this had made her father laugh,
his wonderful gruff, affable laugh

Billy loved that laugh – she heard it so many times,
loved the laugh lines around his deep blue eyes,
loved his deep baritone voice

this journey was both special and sombre
she had been given the responsibility of
taking him back to their special place
that place in the sun, in the wind, in the peace
that place where dreams came to life,
a place for dreams

she placed his ashes, with a daughter's tenderness,
into her saddlebag, the one with the tie-down still intact

it would be their last ride together,
but she knew it would not be the last time
they would be together

she looked down at her mother's
green eyes, puffy and red
a trail of tears carved into her weathered face

'i'll be back in a few days, don't worry,
Dad wanted me to do this – it was his last request'

with that she tightened the straps on her father's old
cowboy hat, like the one James Stewart wore in *Winchester '73*,
stains and scrapes all in the right places

turning Bella toward the river valley
was her signal – they flew with the wind
like an arrow flying true
until they were out of sight

then easing into a nice steady pace
they followed the trail her father had shown her
all those years ago

Billy's tears had turned to determination a few days back,
in that sterile hospital room
her father said to her privately, because he knew she would understand:
'all is good in the world, i had a good life
and, it's okay i leave; it's my time'
the spirit of those few words helped to ease her sorrow

the sun was beginning to set when she crested a high rocky rise
from there she could see their special place, and

in a way that only she knew –
tomorrow was going to be a happy birth day

Reconciliation / Conciliation

this is what i know

reading about people
talking about reconciliation
and some kind of truths
whose truths – their truths
they deal with their ancestors'
mistakes, their governments and
their churches – their doctrines
praise the Lord

watching people discuss
the findings of the TRC
and how they're going to disseminate
to the masses – what masses
who wants to listen to them talk
they do – they did this for themselves
to make themselves feel better
using their colonized language
to re-conciliate injustices

listening to all the experts
dissecting all the information
from all the stories and all
the video and tapes and
transcripts and photographs
going back to before
and then trying to start over
over – again and again

many times our people
been through all this red tape

and bureaucracy and promises – promises
to do things better and to reconcile
the differences – Wovoka did
a Ghost Dance to conciliate his truths
and the 7th calvary killed 290 Sioux, 1890
all those many years ago
on that lonely plain

what do i know about the truths
i was born away from it all
i was raised in a dominantly white town
up in the northern bush land
a few comings and goings on
of my people, but hardly
enough to notice that we lived on
Bannock Avenue – where Mom made bannock

then the day came – the oil companies came
and they came and they took away the land
that we lived on – they kicked
us out of our homes – they bulldozed
our homes to the ground so we wouldn't
go back there and the RCMP
with their guns and tear gas
made sure we stayed away – what the fuck!

so many truths and no one listens – who hears
not enough hearts – not enough compassion
not enough support and the politicians
write new policies – make new legislation
they believe what they do
believe that they know what's best then
they line up to talk to the reporters
to report what they did
and years later – still – nothing

TRUTH and re-conciliation
do we want to go back to when
it was better, well – that would take
us back to before the white man
we're the only ones who can
re-conciliate, but we don't want to
live all the atrocities – over, again
we don't want to lose our children
like the lost thousands whose voices are

s i l e n t . . . .

The Dark Hours

in the dark hours
i reach out for You
i want to touch Your hands
touch Your heart
touch Your soul

in the dark hours
i climb the ladder
to Your outstretched arms
remove the nails and
take You off the cross

in the dark hours
just before the light
kisses the morning dew
i cover Your body
with an earthly blanket

Crosses at the Crossroads

standing at my crossroads
wondering if it all makes sense

dreams and hopes wait for me
inside my memories

the crosses that i've carried
and left at that intersection.... rust and rot

my destiny vibrates on a hazy summer horizon
dandelion seeds float above red-stained fields

the books remember   the pages i've earmarked
their thoughts still live in me, through me

my father taught me something of life
fight the battle, be your own man

my mother made bannock and rabbit stew
and fixed my worn-through moccasins

"breakfast is ready," and the sweet sound
of her homemade pancakes and bacon cooking

if you fly fast enough you will see
the past lives in the future

if a Thunderbird calls for you
be careful where it may take you

the Athabasca River seduced my imagination
Australia taught me to walk with my ancestors

New York insisted i listen when Vincent
talks about the light of heaven

to live in my past is to dance
amongst the Lilies of the Field

from that first day remembered and the last
i fight the urge to go back, to live it again

yet, needing to touch those stories
i do, i do travel emphatically through time

my brothers carry their crosses
racing for the best seat at the kitchen table

Roland and i swim in the reeds
along the muddy banks of the Snye

i cry out, "take me back sweet dreams
take me back!" i close my eyes and levitate

each time is different, different voices
a bear pillages a blueberry pie from our kitchen window

no matter the pain i'd live it again
i'd run carefree forever along our secret paths

chasing butterflies and bumblebees
to the top of that river's perilous cliff

i'd fall into her arms, lose myself in her infinity
in the dreaminess of her blue-green eyes

golden sunlight descends through leaves
mixing with the songs of the forest

songs of the day mixing with those
songs of the coming night

metaphors on metaphors within
metaphors belonging to time immemorial

the crosses melt into the puddles
along the ditches at the crossroads

one more look, memorizing how to get back
i turn and carry them all with me

walking into the painted city
following the path of Rilke's panther

The End of the Trail

beaten down and shattered
little bits and pieces of me have fallen
into cracks on the floors of all the places i have been
i can see, from where i stand, through the windows
the world in variations and degrees of grey
through stained, broken shards, holding tough
only time, and insects, are the witnesses now
no human visitors

the cold wind flows easily in
past the jagged edges of the panes
and cuts through layers of skin
cutting through to tear
at the heart
of my soul

the house where i used to live
still lives in my imagination   it has
weathered the forces of nature and man
the wooden siding has cracked beyond repair
where pools of grey on all their surfaces
lead to streaks of grey   they look
like divided rivers of time flowing away
haphazardly zigzagging along
too many to count
around all 4 walls
looping back
only to bump
into themselves

even the chimney has cracked and broken
river stones that we hand-picked many years before

have tumbled, crashing to earth, silently i guess
to lie in a long-forgotten dead flower bed

so, in the twilight of my life
i'm here at the end of a lonely road
all by myself in a beautiful winter landscape
the sun is shining and i'm taking photographs
of tracks where a Fisher has been sliding
feeling like i've come full circle
back to my youth

no longer wanting to use a gun, i carry a camera now
only wanting to photograph wild beasts, and
to spend a little bit of time with them

nearing the end of my life
here alone in the bush, i realize
what my ancestors must have realized
this is a good place to be, a good place to live
and a good place for the rest of time
whether in this life, or
in the next

Two Ravens

2 big ravens
in the tallest tree
on the highest branches
squawking, like a couple of truckers
can be heard for kilometres

for Harriet and Harry, it was
love at first sight, forever together

50-ish children

now in their twilight years
their bones ache – it is harder to fly
maybe, i am just projecting

they want to share their truths

"do you speak Raven?"
i asked myself
or did i hear someone or something ask me
"no, but i wish i could."

i imagine what a raven has to say, often
i imagine they are kind of a funny bird
yet, serious when they have to be

a biting social commentary on environmental concerns – perhaps
followed by proud anecdotes of their children
then, there's a new fast-food drive-thru opening soon
excitement, at all the possibilities – that's what i'm thinking

"they are talking to me"
my ancestors told me to listen

the tree stands beside a mythological waterway
with a rusty wrought-iron fence growing into its side
holding it from falling, with the erosion, into the river

the fence is a remnant from when my great-grandfather used to live
    there
my grandfather told me the stories – his name was Harry

i smile as i walk toward them
i gave them their names, it's a personal thing
a kind-of jest – something they would do, i think

the Ravens love their tall old perch
they have been using it for 13 or so years
well, that's as long i've been going back there

i see them on those days
i walk down that hidden bush path toward my secret spot

it's nice to know they are there
talking to me – we are good friends now

i look up and say, "i too, have things to say!"

the leaves have begun to change colour
and once again, i am concerned for my old friends
there is a bite in the air, but i am warm, wearing
my nice new camo jacket with canada-goose down

i walk slowly now – my bones ache
mostly my ankles and my knees

i touch the tree
in the same spot
i have been touching for years

i have a secret agreement with that once-great tree
this i share, only with my dark-feathered friends

i look up, they are watching me, their heads crooked
partly upside down, partly backwards

from their perch, they call down to me
in low guttural croaks and gaggles

i am curious to know what they say
always, sounds like: "welcome back my friend,
how have you been, where have you been?"

i love the view from this spot
i can see a long way, both up and down the river
it speaks to me
just like i imagine it did for my grandfather and his father

i stand silent for an hour or so
listening to the sounds around me
listening to my friends above me
looking at the view
that old view that my great-grandfather knew

a young Raven flies close
its wings swoosh
with a soft whistling sound

one of the children, i presume

"hello," says i, then i croak out a few Raven sounds too
he seems to like that

Harriet and Harry croak out a soliloquy of sorts
and the young one carves back and upwards, landing partway up the tree

over the years, i've met all of the family, and
i feel like an adopted uncle – i'm happy and comfortable with that

the Ravens have been talking to me quite a lot today
and through an osmosis of time a metamorphosis has taken place

each time i understand more of what they are saying

it's time   i begin to walk back to my truck
i turn for a quick look at the river
then up to my friends

my heart is happy
my soul is satisfied
my mind is clear

as i disappear down the trail, walking slowly into the forest
i hear my 2 old friends squawking

The Biggest   FIRE   Ever!

the big, big billowing black clouds of smoke
growing bigger, bigger every second, and higher – higher

i can see from my deck, the deep, dark, black bulging clouds growing
    5, 10, 15 km high
60 km away and it feels like those ominous clouds are just over the hill

my heart is racing, racing, beating erratically, faster – faster
and my nerves feel like they are rubbed raw – RED raw

i pace inside the house, then outside, then inside
my mind bounces, i sense and feel protons and electrons heating up

i'm worrying about my home, worrying about my grandkids; i've got
    them with me
and i'm wondering what we're going to do

i'm worrying about our community and all our homes
i ask my neighbours and my cousins – what are we doing?

i talk to the chief, then to the First Nation CEO, i suggest
we prepare for the scores of people coming, refugees

refugees from my old hometown, Fort McMurray, modern refugees
coming to our village, a long steady line of vehicles fill up our homes

fill up our Elders' centre, fill up our youth centre
fill up our band hall and fill up our school gymnasium

filling up our tiny hamlet where 450 Aboriginal people normally live
    a quiet life
while just to the south and to the west the fire rages – RAGES

R A G E S on and on and on and burns and eats and kills
and moves and grows, bigger, bigger – BIGGEST FIRE EVER!

moose die, deer die, squirrels die, bears die
pines and spruces die, poplars and willows die, spring flowers die

bees die, butterflies die, blackbirds die, robins die
wolves die, foxes die and even coyote dies too

i can imagine them all running or flying with no escape, fires in front
    of them
then they turn away, fires there too – and smoke, black smoke

then they turn again and run back – they go left, then right, then left
confusion and ultimately – smoke inhalation – they all burn to death!

and as the fire rages on – will people die? will my friends die?
will my neighbours die? will McMurray burn down? will our village
    burn down?

parents wonder if their kids are safe at school
should they go get them? yes, hurry – H U R R Y!

husbands and wives at work wonder where their families are
wonder where their kids are, wonder where – where? they race home!

they are phoning and texting and tweeting and messaging and
    Facebooking
i got messages from friends asking if there is room at my place; they
    are coming

i say yes come here, i am getting things ready, i am cleaning the house
i got things to do, people show up and are still coming – bring food i say!

friends' houses are in the path of the fire, some are burning
they are in their cars, in their trucks, they've grabbed what they could

they've grabbed photo albums and computers and passports and
  records of things
and deeds of their homes, insurance papers; their homes may burn
  down – burn down!

they grab mementoes and all kinds of things, things with meanings
  attached to them
pictures, paintings, blankets, toys, statues and even whatever's near
  the door

tens of thousands of people all getting out of town, all at one time,
  the same time
the roads clogged, the highways jammed – one highway south, one
  north

then we see on YouTube the near misses, the fire churning, the fire
  laughing
the fire dancing beside vehicles as they all drive on one road – south
  or north

over the cars and trucks the fire jumps and flies and floats and soars
over the cars and trucks over the roads – over the rivers

from one neighbourhood to another
from one community to another, then – to the next town?

we know that McMurray is burning, houses are burning
trees burning, buildings burning, many neighbourhoods burning

this could happen to our community, our little hamlet
we need to do something, we need to get to work

cut down the trees, bulldoze the trees, create a firebreak
create a barrier around our community and then hope and pray

people are watching the smoke, guessing what is happening

guessing what's going to happen, guessing – guessing

our little community is abuzz with worry and questions
what to do? what are we going to do? what are they doing?

who is going to do something? what the fuck and holy shit
this is bad, is McKay going to burn too?

Those big, billowing clouds of smoke, climbing higher – higher
every second, THE BEAST is burning, burning – bigger – B I G G E R . . . .

From Hamburgers and Fries

the discussion turned from hamburgers and fries
to food for thought
in a busy fast-food restaurant
i sat with an old friend
excited by f-stops
and a lack of aberrations
and groups of elements
full frame sensors or APS-C
or something else that may be just as good
for just what's needed

the food tastes great
it's my regular fare

whirring voices around us
are softened by our talk
of giant drones
lifting cameras
hundreds of feet
taking images integrating the overall picture
consideration for composition and light
and negative and positive spaces
helping us focus
on subjects
from different angles

it feels nice just to sit
with an ingenious, dexterous mind

i hear the wind
buffeting the window
but inside the AC fans are working overtime

i put on a jacket
to protect against
the double cold front,
brrrrr....

a great conversation
brought us together

there's a couple of women
sitting across from us
who get up and leave
wearing spandex
their tight little butts
broadcasting
        "look at me!"
yes, they're cute, of course
it's hard not to notice

our thoughts flow easily
considering the many suggestive abstractions

it's not a French back-alley cafe we're in
nor an Italian restaurant along the Mediterranean
no, we're not in the food court of the MET in NYC
nor in the Blue Bottle Coffee House in San Francisco
we're not drinking absinthe or eating Kobe beef sliders
it's just water from the tap and a charbroiled 8-ounce burger
served by a Filipina lady with a nice smile
on paper plates and in paper containers
that slip nicely into a big garbage bin beside the door

2 artists sitting
talking about life and work – art

In Our Kitchen

John Wayne was eating breakfast in the kitchen
he was the fourth stranger
to be sitting there this month
when i woke up
so i was not really that surprised

bacon, eggs, beans, and homemade toast
my mother's favourite, and ours too
the sizzling bacon sound and its smell wafting through my bedroom
made me crawl out of bed

fresh off the trail, his shirt and vest still dusty
i heard his horse outside

Mom and Dad had a
"make yourself at home" policy
and of course, everyone did

last week there was some fellow
from somewhere north, Alaska i think

Mr. Wayne had made bush coffee just the way my grandfather did
there was something familiar i liked about that
i poured myself a nice hot cup
before sitting at our heavy wooden homemade table
cut from 100-year-old Jack pine

i noticed his big sweat-brimmed hat
hanging on the hook on the wall
typical kind of cowboy hat

then i noticed his boots, amongst ours

big, with the pointed toes scuffed past repair
probably, i thought, from kicking cow patties
i chuckled to myself

in his gruff smoke and whisky voice, he said,
"howdy Pilgrim,"
now that's a bit like a cliché i thought, so i replied:
"i reckon i'm doing fine pardner, ummm, i mean Mr. Wayne"
i don't know what came over me at that moment
"just call me John," he said
when i looked up at him he had a big grin
he took a sip from his steaming cup

just about that time i heard faint footsteps
my brothers and sister were finally awake too
and soon there would be no food left
i jumped up, loaded my plate
started eating – shovelling it down
food was fair game in our house
even if it was on someone else's plate

Mom walked in the back door, at that moment
with a basket full of clean clothes
something looked out of place – oh yeah....
it must have been that she didn't have that mussed-up housewife look
her hair was done nicely
she was wearing her new red flowered summer dress
the one she had ordered from the Sears catalogue last week
that made me smile

John stood up as she entered the kitchen
he said, "let me help you with that ma'am"
of course, Mom said that it was okay
looking at me and at the clothes
taking them into the front room
i knew then what my first job of the day was

i ate slower and filled my cup again
and poured John another

Mom said, "Dad's got the boat ready,
John, you can head down anytime you like"
and to me she said that i was to go along too
but only after i finished the clothes
i shovelled down the rest of my food
Mom knew how much i loved his movies
she also knew that it would be handy for Dad to have me around

over the years many folks have made themselves
at home in our kitchen
my mom and dad would have it no other way

and as a kid there would be many more mornings
of strangers in the kitchen
but never anyone, with a dusty hat or big cowboy boots
or a horse in the backyard

My Favourite Golf Course

i teed up my ball on the 1st box
where my great-grandfather
lived in a small log cabin
that he built for his family
who watched the aurora borealis
on cold clear winter nights
wearing moosehide jackets
lined with Timber Wolf fur.

i hit my ball down #2's long fairway
where i used to walk on paths
overgrown with ferns
with young fiddleheads
stopping to pick a few
to take home
to my grandfather
who loved to fry them
in a nice bit of butter and salt.

i made a long curving putt on the 7th green
where i used to hunt squirrels
with childhood friends
that we cooked on a small fire
because we were hungry
and because we liked
the taste of the meat
when it was cooked
over open flames.

i stopped at the snack shack
where i used to set snares
to catch rabbits

for a pot of rabbit stew
with potatoes and vegetables
that i would sop up with
a fresh slice of bannock

    on the 12th my approach shot landed near the hole
where i used to pick raspberries
with my mother
who used them to make pie
that was so good
that it felt like
we tasted heaven
right here on earth

   i hit my drive into the river on 16
where my brother and i fished
with my father
when we were just knee high
to a baby bear
who wanted to steal
the fish we threw
onto the shore

    i looked for a ball hit into the bush on the last
where i made love to my first girlfriend
with the freckles and a pretty smile
who opened my world
to the glory of manhood
on a late spring /
early summer evening
so long ago

A Stroke of the Brush

i told them to give me two weeks
and i'll do a pastoral scene, perhaps of

the fading sunny mountain peaks with sporadic clouds above
hints of the coming days, my excitement, troubling

a typical scene, yet with a distinct difference....
3 trolls on a red bridge, waiting, in the early morning shadows

while each unique, they had a strange similarity
upon their heads were worn-out yellow sombreros

they have lived alongside empathetic humans for hundreds of years,
    secluded
secret mountainous environment, over time we accepted each other's
    quirks

from afar it appears they might be celebrating a special holiday
humans yearly guess this event as the trolls have remained quite
    mysterious

a sesquicentennial, perhaps, yet time runs under the bridge, steadily
the seasons were loved equally, by all creatures

if you listen to the soft swishing of the river currents
you can damn near recognize the dreams of civilizations long past

you can hear their words, written in time, sent into space and back
echoes from Proxima Centauri, if you listen to their legends

the possibility of an early end, we don't know for sure, it's a feeling
humans speak about it over cocktails, however no one truly understands

coffee and pastries, and natural foods of sorts, all are welcome
selections for big folks and little friends, start the conversation

one epoch has led to another, people have heard the scientific musings
the time to save ourselves was long ago, experts expressed their concerns

i sit at my easel with brush in hand, full of anticipation
my head filled with ideas, my world view ever changing

a single brush stroke hasn't enough power to move an entire world
or change two entire points of views and ways of lives, but – let's see....

Don't Get Me Started

don't talk to me about the weather
don't ask me to go for lunch

don't get me started

when you haven't called in years
and you heard i was the CEO

don't get me started

have you heard the news?

let's talk about

my grandfather's fresh bannock
butter melting into its hot soft insides

now that's a good topic

a robin's song, heard
as twilight crests the dark hills

4 White Horses

sometimes dreams of
spinning galaxies and fading light years
nebulous starbursts in lazy rivers
     EXPLODE
thoughts of times and generations
heavenly songs of courageous adventures
     of golden suns
     everywhere
     blasting thru a cerebral stratosphere

somewhere tiny spheres of light
born of the most distant stars swirl
     colours of destruction
     and creation
     encapsulations of knowledge
rainbows of invisible words
     patterns in a full colour scheme
     tiny luminary eruptions
     all whispering to my soul

somehow promises of life
on volatile currents of solar winds
flow through our bodies
of carbon, hydrogen and oxygen
non-laminar flow creating
     a hundred thousand
     almost imperceptible
     moments – thoughts – memories
caressing the deepest part of the spiritual

four white horses gallop straight at me
i barely have time to jump out of the way

grabbing the rail of the chariot they pull
i clasp the reins
a mixture of tumbling light and shadows and dust
trails as we race through the darkening sky
my emotions are etched on the heavens
      consequences of my ancestors and of all humanity
      ascend with us

By the Tailings Pond

i'm writing a poem just for you
trying to paint a nice pastoral scene
of my people living by the river

you may like to hear this story
of those forgotten special places and times
where my people and family gathered

if possible you may be able to taste
the blueberries and cranberries picked not far from there
then boiled with a few of Granny's favourite ingredients – delicious

perhaps the smell of moose meat cooking in a cast-iron skillet
would cause you to salivate and your belly to rumble
the sound of the meat and fat sizzling like music

bannock driving taste buds into a frenzied state
enriched flour and refined sugar, goodness gracious
with butter and moose meat or butter and strawberry jam – mmmmn

then unexpectedly your mind registers the soft warm wind
flowing down into and along the river valley
as you watch children playing at the water's edge

then a few ducks floating near the far bank catch your eye
and you subconsciously drift off to where that crazy squirrel is
    chattering
reminding you of the young black bear who tried to sneak into camp
    last night

all our grandparents are sitting in the shade, just out of the sun
slightly in the trees at the top of the long sloping river's rise
smoking tailor-mades, drinking tea and sharing stories

they're talking about Sue, pregnant with Johnny's baby
and the great deal they got from the hudson's bay man
and the Tea Dances on Christmas and New Year's Day

Every so often Grandpa would stand and shout at the kid
who would be in the mud about to jump into that fast-flowing river
or throwing rocks into the water close to where the kids are –
    "careful, careful!"

now and then a wind swirls from a different direction
bringing back the smell of meat and bannock and berries
sizzling and baking and boiling on small fires in the camp

suddenly there's the crack of my father's axe – chopping wood
i see through the trees my mother bending over – stirring something
i'm not hungry yet, but i know that it'll be supper soon – excitement
   growing

perhaps you don't know these sounds and smells, but
you may remember similar moments in your family's home
on lazy Sunday afternoons, after coming back from church – amen

as a skinny brown boy, i remember those times so very well
standing silently, halfway between the river and the Elders
looking around and up and down the river for miles and miles

i know now how special those days were
yet somehow, i had a sense of it when i was standing there
so, let me finish this poem – let me finish that picture

i went for a boat trip on that river just a few years back
and drove past that place, it felt like i was in slo-mo
it's surrounded now – on 3 sides – by a mountainous tailings pond

the memories still live there – in my heart
i can see and feel those moments
as i write this poem for you

My Own Private Hell....

i'm in my own private hell living
here in my old home
town beside the river of my
dreams flowing north

evaporating into the dark cosmos of my
imagination touching eternal damnation
where all of eternity watches today as
i struggle

making ends meet
where the brush touches the canvas
scratching canvas   that sound i love, scratching

an artist of some repute not looking for that
kind of public affection conducive to

egomaniacal narcissistic tendencies of most
but wanting a monetary reward so i can purchase a can of beans

yet i hunger for an emotional restitution of spirit
calling me back from the darkness which
i love more than i should

my heart leads me home
and i put my hat in that familiar place by the door

Sometimes, the Darkness....

sometimes, the darkness
        in the middle of the night
                is darker than it should be
my heart can't hold on anymore
        and now a deep cut in my wrist
                drips with dark, cherry-coloured blood
there's a delicate trail
        of blood on the freshly cut lawn
                from my back door down to the creek
i'm looking back at the light in the kitchen
        wondering if this is a good idea
                but no one has heard my cries
the voice in my head is strong
        it tells me to keep walking
                as i stumble over exposed roots
i hear the crickets and frogs talking
        to their own friends and mates
                and to some kindred water nymphs
woodland spirits are hidden from view just beyond
        the light of dimly flickering fireflies
                floating between branches and over the open water
i am enticed to sit at the end of my short, weathered dock
        i listen for my creature friends
                they have called me out tonight
but i guess my presence
        made them nervous
                and all has gone deathly silent
yet, a half light from the half moon
        wiggles off the ripples of the creek
                the surface of its water is calming
i see a half-clothed mage floating inches above the water
        waving for me to come to her
                my imagination is overactive again

her invitation gives me something to consider
        at least my late-night friends are here with me
                a firefly suddenly zigzags through this misty vision
breaking the hypnotic spell for a split second
        giving me a chance to ask myself if this is someone
                or something that i should listen to
but the self-pity is overwhelming
        and i loathe myself for having such dark thoughts
                on such a beautiful, full night
the light of a firefly disappears
        and all that remains, the splash of a fish
                then the hollow sound of water lapping against rusty metal
it's my father's old green, two-toned '57 Chevy
        that we pushed into the river over a quarter century ago
                giving me the sense of a lifetime flying by
i'm reminded of 4 mischievous neighbourhood kids
        running through the bush with bows and arrows
                on similar summer nights, all those years ago
happy memories of promises and hope
        that have lived here along this water's edge
                for far too long, all by themselves
i tried to reach those stars
        that i thought i could touch
                when i climbed old Walton's Mountain
but here i am, sitting on these grey planks
        stained by the puddle of blood at my side
                surrounded by crickets and frogs and fireflies
i look up from that red puddle
        to the faint image of that lonely moon
                partially hidden by overhanging branches and leaves
i've been sitting there for long enough
        that the crickets and frogs are talking again
                a small sense of happiness slips into my thoughts
i turn to the right and push myself up from the dock
        i hear my knees creak as i stand
                it sounds eerily like crickets talking

something whispers to me at the back of my mind
       and i look over my left shoulder
             and catch a glimpse of that beautiful mage
such a beautiful image that time has created
       one of her with an outstretched hand, holding an apple
             but i can't be so sure; she has disappeared too soon
i can see the light coming from the kitchen
       it's not as far away as it looks
             i take a small step forward with my good foot first
a chill runs up my spine
       as my bare feet touch the dewy grass
             i continue to walk back to the old house
my pace is careful and calculated
       i feel cool dewdrops running between my toes
             giving me a strange notion of urgency
i also feel the softness of the soil
       and the warmth of the earth
             my evening walk has heightened my senses
this is the 3rd time that i've made this walk
       in this depressed state of mind
             it may be the last, that's hard to say
the kitchen light hurts my eyes
       as i open the back door to the house
             i take one more look, over my right shoulder, at the half moon

I've Lived the Best I Can

i tried to live life the best that i can
which seems amazing, from where it began
we lived on the other side of those tracks
where so many have fallen through the cracks
two blocks from main street and just down the hill
i have fallen too, but through strength of will
i climbed from that hole, clinging to my roots
sometimes, wearing my father's worn-out boots

sitting here it's hard to know where to start
for, in each of their ways they played a part
with friends, i played baseball in the rock-filled fields
then next day we'd make wooden swords and shields
on sunny days, we'd swim in our river
the stories of them, all kind of differ
in those vague and magical sorts of ways
they sneak back in on those long lazy days

our home was built by our own callused hands
next to the tallest pines and poplar stands
let's talk a bit about my neighbours now
musings of some, i try to disavow
but those old days keep pulling me back in
a few steps from that original sin
and though i remember them all fondly
their faces slip into a darkened sea

one friend said he'd protect me to the end
he's in jail now for killing two women
his brother dealt drugs in the big city
he was shot in a field, such a pity
a so-called friend kicked my dad in the head

his car rolled on a dark road, now he's dead
his brother boxed, he had a few defeats
and he too died there on those city streets

ten years ago, one girl who lived next door
talked to me of her family's horror
then this boy who came to our side of town
with his slingshot made a girl lift her gown
then there was Billy   forget him? never
he went boating and drowned in our river
i'd talk about more, you get the picture
they're all a different kind of life's fixture

of course, i should speak of my family
i prayed God would listen and set me free
my father and his friends, alcoholics
this made my mom mad; they had no ethics
she was angry   took it out on us
yelling and screaming, we learned how to cuss
the days of my youth were often dreadful
so i tried for years to break the circle

i think of them in black and white sometimes –
of those who passed, victims of their own crimes
i remember them, their pains and glory
they lived next door and they had their story.
so, every now and then, when i look back
to our old long-gone home, that weathered shack
the place that we all built with our young hands
i think.... i've lived my life the best i can

I Was Looking at a Painting

i was looking
at a river
in a painting
and it was moving, running
it must have been
this trick of mind
that reminded me
of a boy
sitting on the roof
of his parents' house
surrounded by the shavings
of the wood
of the bow
and the arrows
he was making and just
as he looks up
at the sky
he sees the wind blowing
molecule-like waves
across the horizon
reminds me
as i write these few lines
of a few paintings
of my troubled friend –
Vincent
whose skies move effortlessly
into the spaces between
my soul and logic
between his world and mine
and i say unto you
reader / viewer
consider the cosmos

and the stars
when the troubled skies
of my old friend
rouse your mind
to run wild
when the river
in a painting
runs into
your imagination
and touches your
heart!

Jelly Jar Logic

living in a jelly jar,
floating on a beam of light,
psychedelic transcendental thoughts
race through piles of mental junk
looking for a place to land
is an ancient white unicorn
carrying multicoloured trade beads
speaking with my ancestors
then, a knight of the round table
grabs mighty Excalibur
cuts the smoky air
while a rock 'n' roll band
plays a backbeat for a singing nun
making time with 3 vestal virgins
where preachers sermonize
on a topic of acid-free rain

now look behind the light show
you'll find a red ball rolling and
bouncing down the street
where 2 naked bodies
in the distance, between
here and the hill,
are entwined in
passionate verbal intercourse
stopped at a green light
at the corner of Haight and Ashbury
in a crowd of stoned-out people
riding in a black convertible
being driven by a
book-touting English professor
is a young impressionable
long-haired poet

scantily clad women dance
in and along an ancient maze
urged on by electric symphonic music
filtered through newly budded flowers
leading the dancers
away from a conformist society
of grey-suited monkeys
carrying their black satchels
filled with pages on pages
of contracts and memorandums
that indicate that it's okay
to steal Indigenous water rights
finding themselves being led
by a bearded man
wearing a tan-coloured gown
looking like Jesus of Nazareth

a young man walks through hot coals
to lie down on a bed of nails
as a fire serpent
curls up under the bushes
of dried-out branches
trying to hide his frustration
over the lies of political gorillas
pounding their chests
yelling out righteous obscenities
about the ills of society
and how they're going to change
legislation and make policies
that'll better the world
and change the status quo
looking through the curved glass
of a half-empty jelly jar

Red Turns to Black

deep down in the earth,
red blood turns to black
their stories of birth,
lost now, must come back

they hunted the hills,
rested by waters,
their strengths and skills,
their sons and daughters.

i found their stories
still live in our hearts,
tales of their glories
are told with our arts

i see what they saw,
i walk where they walk,
a land deadly raw
where ghosts rarely talk

but all that's been said,
and all that i've known,
and all that we've read,
bleached white to the bone

my blood is their blood,
impressions of time
encased in the mud,
a lost paradigm

i stand on the edge
of life's precipice,

with a silent pledge
to fill this abyss

rip open my chest,
you'll see their heartbeats,
i'll give it my best
to speak of their feats.

out there on our lands,
where earth holds our blood,
a vulgar peace stands,
waits for a great flood

their stories i'm told,
creations of mind,
in this body, i hold
the truths of mankind

let their spirits fly
through eternity,
wash away "the lie,"
give back dignity.

from first breath to last,
they will live through me,
i'll speak of the past;
i'm now their story

so, sit on the dirt
or lie on your back,
it may even hurt
where red turned to black.

The Old Diner

in a dingy old diner
the real old past
and the past
met

it was their annual supper
they got together to talk
and to consider
stuff

the diner lay on the outskirts
of a dusty old town
near a flickering
light

it was at the old crossroads
of those north and south
and east and west
byways

they hadn't talked
for a long time
it had gone by
fast

they loved this greasy spoon
with the old '50s decor
bright and cheery
busy

they sat in a warm corner
beside the big windows

on worn-out
chairs

the old past ordered tea
with a lump of sugar
the past   coffee
black

at the next table quietly sat
two old grey ladies and
two old grey men
smiling

quickly leaving the diner
through double doors
a young couple
laughing

as their conversation commenced
the wind picked up battering
the weathered window
pane

the past started reminiscing
"do you remember when?"
but old past changed to
"Ozymandias"

"Oh, not this again, not him!"
the past knew then
he was headed to
Yeats.

and so as most conversations go
one thought leading to the next
words flung around
convincingly

all of a sudden there was dead silence
everyone turned to see   walking in
was old man Clemens and
Frost

both of these old word-wizards
looked to the corner table
as they sat down
alone

the special was Grandma's meatloaf
which both ordered
and to start
soup

they both talked in hushed voices
not wanting to disturb
the folks who sat
nearby

as the minutes turned to hours,
their talk turned to years
it had that feel of
age

the Sunday night special was tasty
it filled them both nicely
so they ordered
pie

then just before midnight
they split the bill happily
got up and walked
out

if you were there that night
and watched them leave
you'd see true
friendship

they walked out to the corner
and shook each other's hands
one went east   the other
west

on that dingy old diner
on a creaky old sign
was a faded word:
"welcome!"

Ghosts Along the Highway

the ghosts along the highway
stand along the edges of the road
somewhere between here and there,
staunch reminders of the past

they seem to always be there
looking to hitch a ride or to say.... "hi"
and they're heading the same way i'm heading,
especially on a late night like this

on a long, lonely stretch of highway,
on a night with a full moon, partly cloudy,
with drifting dispossessed mists, laden with memories,
i'm all alone with my thoughts, again

i'm getting near to where i have to turn,
where i have to slow down, near that graveyard,
no zipping past this one; it's at the turn in the road,
my mind keeps saying.... "don't think about them."

i'm getting that feeling at the back of my neck,
hairs are standing, as waves of chills sweep up,
i've committed to this route, no going back,
i've chosen this route, or has it chosen me?

there it is, i am trying not to look,
i don't want to get hooked into looking,
i don't want to see that which is there,
but i do, for just a brief second or two

my mind churns like a witch stirring its brew,
it reminds me of all my friends, long gone,

who have lost their lives along those lost highways,
many of them passing alone to the other world

i think back to my old friend and foe, Lambert
we had some good times and there were some bad,
but there he stands watching me go by, watching,
my thoughts slip back to when we were just kids

then there's that place where i last talked to Gary
though he lost his life on another stretch of a forgotten road,
that place where we last talked reminds me to think of him,
and of that tree where his life was violently ended

and always, there's that one place where my brother left us
it's a special place in this world that belongs only to him,
it's on a long sweeping curve where memories of him come back to me
there he is standing in his uniform, high on the steps, saying.... "goodbye."

the drive past the graveyard of my thoughts is a long one,
and along that road, between the places that are here and there, are "them,"
my old friends along with those of my family who have gone before
at those places that belong only to them, i greet them with.... "hello."

the ghosts along the highway, along those lonely edges of time,
standing among the mists of the night, or sometimes in the shade of
   the day,
stand as a reminder of the past, but more as a counsel for the present
those ghosts along the highway are family and are all good friends of
   mine

Hot Pea Soup

seems like life falls into place with a tasty bowl of hot pea soup,
sitting on a cozy chair nestled up to a quaint brown table,
looking out picture windows at the corner of Bleecker and 6th,
at hurried people who walk by heading to places in their minds

seems like life falls into place sitting with my delightful lover,
lost in conversations over a tasty bowl of hot pea soup
on that first fall day, a chilling wind is blowing in from the north,
pressing pedestrians to move quicker to their destinations

seems like life falls into place with sounds of Chopin played overhead,
basking the bistro in tender timbres of Nocturne, Opus 9,
devouring hot pea soup, perfectly enriched with salt and spices,
relieving our weary minds and enticing our bodies to rest

seems like life falls into place as a couple comes in from the cold
we briefly glance at them as they walk past, sitting not far away,
then we carry on with our conversation about things we've seen
i overhear them order the special of the day.... hot pea soup!

Follow That Raven

an intrepid Raven nudges and urges me – "go closer,
move to the edge of that precipice and look out, look below
see beyond the shadows of the trees and the reflections in the water."

my mind is comforted by the voice in my head – curious thoughts indeed!

touch that Raven and it will embrace you with all the world,
listen to it and it will tell you of the joys of its family,
yet be prepared to feel the angst of its knowledge

it's my grandfather's voice that i am hearing – remembered stories!

follow that Raven to the moon and to the sun, then to the next galaxy,
follow, but beware that when you do, it may drive you crazy,
follow it because Raven wants you to follow.

black feathers remind me of the darkness in the world – and balance

My Living Area....

i came in,
i placed my umbrella, precariously, against the wall,
i hung my coat up to dry....
i put my muddy boots on the rack.

i walked into the living room,
i sunk into the couch, unworriedly, comfortable
i turned on the television....
and watched a movie

The Ice Skater....

and so the skater skates, it's 25 below zero
even within the darkest coldness of the night
when all around are already in their comfortable beds
that icy quietude seems to be an encouraging friend
its peacefulness is calling

and so the skater skates, the snow slowly descending
highlighted here and there by 7 flickering streetlights
where the only witnesses are old poplar trees
and some dark figure walking a block and a half away
their shadows are talking

and so the skater skates, long strides then short
like an old Morse code, communicating with the silent spirits
a sharp turn, or a long languid one, on blades circling
round the inside edges of a square surface
each moment is surprising

and the skater skates alone tonight, challenged simply by an idea
within the distance of her thoughts, a familiar concerto is playing
to be there, on her own, with some enlightened revelations
perhaps the Creator has devised a plan for her
the cosmos is a patient companion

Drive On, Walk On – Dream....

drive on, on, i'll take your lead,
and i will be your friend indeed,
but don't forget, we're a diff'rent breed!

walk on, on and on, yet stop, read and sing,
listen, feel, and see, birds, bugs, bears – ev'rything;
in dark of night, light of day – wisdom for you they bring!

rest now along roaring falls and by a forgotten stream,
but rest because it does your heart well my old friend, Karim....
the world's woes are yours i know, but it does your heart well – to dream!

In a Turquoise World

in your mind, you are free
within a dream world, reality exists,
yet swims around and around

a moment is gone, like life unending,
slipping ever forward, nearing the future,
a supernova blasting outwards, red,
and the blue-green silence implodes

two worlds colliding, becoming one,
uniting forever, forsaking fate
a moment longer and the silvery figure is gone,
leaving behind only sentiment
and the water dancing

Relentless....

the bush
calls me out
calling me, talking to me
always, always, always
relentless

and my favourite spot on the river
where i learned to swim is just around the bend from
where that old eagle sat at the top of that old tree and the lake
where i caught that giant Jack also talks to me, relentless
messages, signs from those
times and places

the world changed again when the white people came to this continent
and reading that in a subtext of a history book in university
upset me because i was not taught any of that
in all my years from elementary
through to high school

it's like our people didn't even exist

as i turned those pages i questioned
how traditions changed and how new traditions emerged when
hunting for a livelihood became trapping for a livelihood, when
the oldest place in a province was a trading post for the hudson's bay
company, an outpost of sorts for a new industry, when
a voyageur named Peter Pond happened upon
a village of "Indians" who used a black sticky
substance to make their canoes
watertight

that little village is ours

surrounded today by huge conglomerates
ripping open the land to take out the riches, the oil
that lays beneath those surfaces where my people hunted, where
we congregated just like our ancestors before at
significant times of the year

where are those favourite places
to pick blueberries or cranberries,
the ones my mother loved to harvest?
dug up!

digging up
ripping apart the land
all those unknown gravesites of my ancestors
graves we didn't know even existed until
a company anthropologist jotted down a footnote
in the minutes of a meeting of mine managers mentioning
something about finding bones, possibly hominid, possibly ancient
in a new section of the mine
sometimes emphasized putting a stop
to production

ripping apart the life
force of the animate

our whole world
changed

corporations gave
us good jobs, sustaining a socio-economic
cultural environment that overrides our sometimes forgotten
innate connection to the land, our land, to a point that
we've become alienated from that landscape
from our history   we've become
in part – "them," but
wait

at that point
our local became global

we have a voice
when companies forget their commitments to the environment
we remind them,
our strong, determined, experienced voices
reminds them

voices in my head, ancestors' voices
our old people   our Elders no longer talk about the past,
they've become displaced stories,
stories displaced for such a long time
that we've become displaced too

i hate to mention this, but
the report from the moccasin telegraph
is that COVID-19 took another
of our Elders

relentless, stories die

removal of the land removes
any evidence that we were a part of the land
essentially, they remove our effectiveness
as stewards of the land

we are not at fault here

winter comes
black mud is covered by white
a land ravaged by time and by oil
hungry entities searching the perimeters
of our traditional lands with
vicissitudes of economic
offerings

politicians play
pivotal roles in the future and the eternal
phantasmagorical fantasies, like sexual ecstasies arising half a
    continent away, or
even oceans away, in boardrooms on the 40th floors are oil company
shareholders designating that the oil resources below
ancient lands far away, far removed, are
more important than the people

spiritual realms erupt again and
again the earth quakes as i walk through the forest
my senses are heightened, alive
reminding me the animate
is real

homogeneity of spirit
of economic realities push us further
and further away from our ancestors to a point where and when
we all need a "Moses" to come and save us from them and
inevitably, from
ourselves

my thought is where would we escape to
i do not want to cross all those deserts,
spend 40 years searching
for our promised land

winter comes
the bush road is opened
our people stream onto the land
is a pristine place that we call home, where
we live our culture amongst the ancestors
living with the plants and animals
talking to us

alas, our favourite place is just beyond the sounds

of those engines, those machines working, relentless to a point,
a breaking point
my people need time to reflect, to count our blessings, to realize that
should we be happy that we have a place
to reflect, a place
to consider ourselves
lucky

we catch fish
we hunt moose
we pick berries
we look at the stars
we watch our children play

and through it all

"our" lawyers fight the battles for us
"our" chief and council decide on what fights to fight, listening to
"our" land, hearing "our" ancestors telling us to stand
"our" ground

enough is enough, but
we also have to know when is enough
enough

we are nothing without the land

our battles are in the courts
we cite the "crown's" responsibility to us
their fiduciary responsibility,
their duty to consult

the battles continue
because golden-collared monkeys in fancy suits
from corporate head offices
from all parts of the world rain down continually

using any means possible including political posturing and sublime
corruptions of office,
promises of economics

we help them,
we help ourselves,
we have a piece of the pie, yet
are we the guardians of the land speaking
behind closed corporate doors

be careful how you
take the land

not so long ago the fur industry died
our way of life ceased, was taken away, taken when well-meaning
environmentalists spray-painted fur coats in London, Paris and New
    York
hurting, my people attacked by the same people who ask for our help
    to save the land
using fancy phrases like anthropogenic climate change, waving placards
shouting obscenities outside corporate head offices

hurt people became destitute
we were once experts at hunting and
trapping   trapped now, we are experts in the oil industry
forced to make hard choices

we go from one tradition
to the next, to the next,
described, delineated, desired
global prospects

yet, the land
continues to speak to us, there's an
innate sense of the sacred, an innate sense of
the animate, a connection to the land that

exists in our people, we are
the land, our bodies
remember

there is something out there, out where
our people can't wait
to get back to

i became a man
under the tutelage of my father
he took me out onto the land, he taught me how to hunt
how to read the signs on and along the trail
and tales my grandfather told me
as i watched the fire in his
pot-bellied wood stove

the moon is full tonight, silent
my community is asleep except for the howling
of reserve dogs and beyond and not far away i hear
the sound of machines as they move earth, relentless, building
tailings ponds, sandy berms holding precariously
the effluent of the rich

relentless conversations in my head
calling to me, calling, innate
animate discussions of

the bush

Let's Talk

so, let us begin

let's talk – Truth and Reconciliation
but first
you can't talk about truth
without talking about all the lies
all the lies of all the governments
from canada's first "right honourable" prime minister
from the first Trudeau to the second
"right honourable," right?....wrong!
let's talk about why they thought they should
"get rid of the Indian problem"
let's talk about the 1969 "white paper"
let's talk about canada's absent leader missing on
the inaugural National Truth and Reconciliation Day
oh no – he wasn't missing, he was on a beach
oh yes – he said he was sorry (that's Aboriginal apology #13)

let's continue talking about truth
talking about all the other lies
of all the churches
let's talk about the thousands of dead Aboriginal children
in unmarked graves all across canada
let's talk about the pope's lack of an apology
about all the dark secrets of his black-robed priests
disciples of destruction and death
have you heard enough yet
do you feel the pain of the Aboriginal people
do you feel some sort of guilt or anger
well we've just started

let's continue

let's talk about education
let's talk about our history
where are the school history books
that recognize that Aboriginal people existed/exist here in canada?
don't get me started, but of course I already have
so, let's continue?

let's talk about our dances
let's talk about our drums
let's discuss ceremony and celebration
but when we do
let's not forget about the 1885 legislation outlawing potlatches
outlawing our cultural practices
let's talk about the "Indian act"
let's talk about the subjugation of our cultures
a blatant subjugation of our peoples
do you get the idea yet?
can you imagine
the angst and pain and suffering and fear and loss and....?
need I say more?
of course, I should

let's continue to talk about education
let's talk about the residential schools
the institutions of genocide
the institutions of assimilation and hate – strong words
some people may be offended
at least that's a reaction

but not as bad as those reactions of priests and nuns
with mantras of their religious doctrines
cut their hair
burn their clothes
beat them and whip them till there's no "Indian" left
lock them up
throw away the keys

get rid of their identity
get rid of their connection to the land
get rid of their connection to their people

stolen children ripped from the arms of mothers
stolen children ripped from the embrace of their communities
stolen children, stolen, crying night after night
crying in the dark and in the day, crying in the shadows
till there was no more crying to be heard – silent, silence
stolen children lie in unmarked graves – everywhere
let's talk about that
lest we forget it was
a war against the children

cbc news just the other day reported
that the rcmp removed a young Aboriginal child from his home
"removed" – tame word compared to what they did
ripping him away from his home
crying and screaming – screaming
screams without hope
the huge officer
in his bullet-proof vest
with his gun at his side
ripping this young person from his home
picked him up, muscles taut imprisoning this little child
the child screaming
the screams
the screams
still echo in my ears

perhaps it is exactly like
all those children
all those many years ago
who were ripped from their families
crying, screaming
the screams, screams

like ghosts wailing in the night
I can only imagine them now
I feel their pain
I hear their cries
time does not erase
time does not heal

shall I continue
does your heart hurt yet?
do your eyes shed any tears? or,
do you try to hold back those tears
do you sit in the dark late at night
thinking, thinking, thinking
about all the stolen children
stolen youth, stolen hope, stolen laughter
and even stolen tears
do your tears sting
do they taste salty
well mine do
mine do

let's continue
let's talk about reconciliation
but, you can't without
talking about racism
you can't without
talking about those stereotypes
in the movies and in the pages of supposed great classics
of drunken Indians, savage Indians
on the streets and in the back alleys

do you want to continue to talk about reconciliation?
do you really or are you tired yet?
do you feel our pain?
do you feel the pain of our ancestors?
do you feel the pain of the children?

do you feel the pain of the mothers
who lost their babies
who never heard from them again
who never knew where they were
who never knew if they were alive
or dead?
do you feel the pain of all those children who lie in unmarked graves?
do you feel their pain?
do you hear their screams – their cries before they died?

and then again
do you feel the pain of the lost red souls incarcerated in white
    prisons, souls who feel no pain?
no pain because their dead souls feel only the nothingness
like zombies – the walking dead barely alive on the streets
do you feel the pain of those
who live in back alleys, in trash bins, in cardboard boxes
who live in the smell of rotting trash?
trash masking the smell of their own rotting flesh, rotting life, rotting
    hope, rotting faith
who live without roofs over their heads
who live in -30 degree weather
who live without understanding why they live like they do
who drink anything to hide their pain and
who shoot up till they blow their heads apart

subjugation and assimilation
shaming and beatings
have done their jobs
some families have no core and the children get lost in their own world
only to find themselves on the streets not knowing why
even years and generations after the fact

reconciliation
let's talk about that
let's talk about the bulldozers on Moccasin Flats

let's talk about the rcmp on Wet'suwet'un land
let's talk about the nwmp who tried to get "rid of the Indian problem"
let's talk about that phrase some more, but first
let's talk about the murdered and missing Indigenous women and girls
let's talk about legislation that continues to subjugate our people
continuing to steal our lands
continuing to rob our people
continuing to negate our dreams
and hope

have you heard enough?
have you had enough?
do you want to do something?

really
do you still want to talk about truth and reconciliation?
if you do
let's talk about healing
let's talk about all of our pains
theirs, yours and mine
let's talk about the drum
let's talk about the dance
about celebrations and ceremony
about differences of culture
about understanding and working together
so much work to do
so much to do

so

let's begin

Acknowledgements

It is so hard to write an acknowledgement because there have been so many people who have influenced me throughout life, who have dreamed with me, journeyed with me, and supported me on this earthly walk. But I will try....

Though I followed a path different than the one they hoped I would, I thank my mom and dad for their words spoken that acknowledged my chosen ways, and for those words unsaid because they knew I travelled to places unfamiliar to them.

Where would I be without those whose patronage recognizes that what I do is important and essential within the realm of our community and culture? Chiefs Dorothy, Jim and Mel: your vision and leadership has given our community and myself the self-esteem to rise above the darkness. David, Nicole, Dave, Chris and Lee: your business acumen and community support impacts all in positive and transcendent ways by showing us that anything is possible.

I say this to all my friends: in each of your own ways, through sharing your aspirations and dreams, I was, and truly am, encouraged to follow my own. Doug and Kevin: all those long late night / early morning conversations – fantastical, esoteric, ethereal or otherwise – helped me journey to imagination. Pierre and Paul: your artistic endeavours have incited my creative perceptions to go where they are meant to go. Justin, Mel and Cliff: interposing life's serious side with laughter has made my walk lighter. Mary, Lisa and Kathy: I understand better now, and I keep trying to be a better man, so thank you for that. And to Karim: the life you've chosen illuminates the greatness of human spirit and gives hope that our world will achieve the greatness it promises to be....

And to all I say: follow your dreams, and your journeys will be the difference!

About the Author

Frederick McDonald is an international, award-winning artist – a painter, poet and photographer – and a member of the Fort McKay First Nation. Fred was born in Fort McMurray and raised in the bush along the Athabasca River, where he was brought up in his parents' traditional hunting and trapping lifestyle. Although he has travelled far and wide, Fred's heart is still with his community and he continues to be an active member of the Fort McKay band. Fred keeps himself grounded through his family. His children and grandchildren are his inspiration for everything he does, and they are his greatest creation.